Whole: 30- Foods Cookbook

Healthy Whole Recipes for Weight Loss

Table of Contents

Introduction

Welcome aboard!

If you are planning to bring a much-needed change in your life, then you have certainly come to the right place.

Are you trying to lose weight for a very long time or is suffering from an unexplainable health condition?

With a revolutionary Whole30 diet, you can witness the most significant change in your life. Food is not just a necessity but is often called our lifeline. What we eat gets reflected in our body in more ways than you can think of. From weight gain to inflammation and change in our metabolic activity to making us prone to diseases like cancer, everything is associated with our diet.

Take the most important journey of your life with us in these next 30 days. In this guide, we will make you familiar with several healthy recipes that can be prepared for breakfast, lunch, and dinner. Also, we will provide in-depth knowledge about the revolutionary Whole30 diet plan and how it can alter your health. Let's get it started!

Chapter 1: What Is Whole30 Diet?

Whole30 is a popular technique and is often termed as a "challenge" to schedule a healthy diet plan for 30 days. Just like any other challenge, it has the same golden rule. If you slip, you start your plan from scratch again. It might sound tough to execute, but not when you can eat some of the most delicious meals in those 30 days.

Whole30 diet plan is not at all about starving yourself to lose weight. In fact, consider it as a learning process (or even an intervention), in which you make peace with a healthy lifestyle.

Ideally, the Whole30 diet plan focuses on diminishing the overall inflammation process in our body. This is done by a combination of elimination diet and paleo diet plan. In this 30-day challenge, you are expected to make a right choice for yourself by consuming the kind of healthy food that would have a positive impact on your life.

The focus of this diet plan is to change the way you consume food. By following a strict 30-day plan, you would be able to see a significant change in yourself. From the way you crave food to its overall taste, the way you consume basic ingredients would be altered.

In a nutshell, a Whole30 diet plan will change your emotional relationship with food, so that you can make a right choice in the future. By following this temporary plan, you can have a permanent change in your life.

What to eat?

It might surprise you, but you can eat almost everything during the 30-day challenge. This is what makes the Whole30 diet plan so different from anything else that you might have tried before.

The principle behind the diet plan is not to starve yourself, so that you can get in shape. Instead, the whole focus is to create a healthy lifestyle. As suggested, you can consume almost every kind of food, including meat, eggs, vegetables (lots of it), fruits, oils, seeds, nuts, cereals, and a lot more.

Focus on more natural and unprocessed ingredients. In this guide, we have come up with plenty of breakfast, lunch, and dinner recipes that will make your job of handpicking just the right amount of ingredients a whole lot easier.

Additionally, you should try to focus on the consumption of macronutrients (proteins, fats, and carbohydrates) as well as micronutrients (minerals and vitamins). While most of the people are able to judge the kind of food items that are rich in carbohydrates and proteins, they usually make a big mistake while selecting fat-rich components.

Most of the people are under a common impression that fats are not healthy for our body. Well, it's not true at all. There are different kinds of fats, and they have the same significance as any other nutrient like protein or carbohydrates.

Before you make your shopping list and a diet plan, make sure that you know the difference between saturated and unsaturated fats.

Saturated fats are ideally not considered a healthy option. They are also known as Trans fat and are found in a solid state. They are not spoilt quickly and have a better shelf life, which is why they are extensively used. Though, they can cause some serious damage to your heart and digestive system. Additionally, they are considered as a primary reason for obesity.

Unsaturated fats, on the other hand, are relatively healthy for your body (if consumed in an ideal amount). They are found in a liquid state and can increase our overall good cholesterol (HDL) level. They have Omega-3 fatty acid, which is extremely good for our body.

Some of the sources of saturated fat are processed butter, margarine, cheese, hydrogenated oil, peanut, fried foods, etc. Unsaturated fat can be found in avocados, walnuts, flax, red meat, naturally processed oils (like olive oil, sunflower oil, soybean oil, canola oil, etc.) and other natural resources.

Now when you know what are the primary things that you should eat during the Whole30 diet plan let's move ahead and see the kind of food items that should be avoided.

What not to eat?

To decrease the inflammation rate and regain your metabolism, you might have to say goodbye to a lot of unhealthy food items. Also, you might have to bring a change in your overall lifestyle as well. Consider the following thoughtful suggestions in mind before you learn how to cook some delicious Whole30 recipes.

- Avoid consuming added sugar or any other artificial sweetener. This includes honey, nectar, maple syrup, coconut sugar, etc. Before buying anything, try to read carefully to know if any item has added sugar or not.

- This one might be a little tough, but you can't consume alcohol during your diet plan. Neither you can have a direct consumption nor can you add it to your food. Also, don't consume tobacco or any other harmful substance.

- No legumes. Avoid peanuts or any other kind of beans (kidney, black, red, lima, etc.). Peas, lentils, chickpeas, and soy products (tofu, miso) should also be consumed less.

- Try to consume a lesser quantity of grains, as they have more starch. Although, it is quite tough to completely avoid rice, corn, wheat, oats, barley, you can always restrict their consumption to a certain level.

- Whenever you are consuming dairy products, be a little cautious. Try to avoid cheese, sour cream, yogurt, or cream. Though, you can consume other sources of unsaturated fat.

- Needless to say, try not to consume MSG or sulfites.

- Say no to junk foods and make sure that you are consuming limited baked goods (muffins, pancakes, waffles, biscuits, pastries, cookies, pizza crust, and so on).

Exceptions

- There are, however, a few exceptions to the above-mentioned list. Feel free to include the following items in your diet.

- Use fruit juices as a sweetener

- Consume clarified butter (or ghee)

- Certain legumes (like green beans, sugar snap peas, snow peas, etc.)

- Vinegar

- Salt

Most importantly, don't weigh yourself or take any measurements during the duration of the Whole30 diet plan. The motive of undertaking a plan like this is not to magically reduce weight. It is all about developing healthy eating habits and harnessing a positive emotional bond with food.

Now when you know what the basic features of a Whole30 diet are, let's dive in a little further and proceed to the next chapter.

Chapter 2: Benefits Of The Whole30 Diet Plan

As stated, the Whole30 diet plan can certainly bring a revolution in your lifestyle. There are almost endless reasons why you should go for this diet plan and experience a diverse consumption of food. The diet plan focuses on providing a complete nutrient palette for you, which comes with a lot of benefits. Some of them are as follows:

- Whole30 diet is one of the easiest plans to execute. Unlike any other diet plan, it won't ask you to starve. Instead, you would learn new ways to cook healthy food.

- By cooking your own meals, there would be no chance of eating adulterated food. Also, it would be quite economical as well.

- There would be no digestive problems. You would be free from stomachaches and other gastric problems related to indigestion.

- Since there would be less sugar and more protein level in your body, you can have a sound sleep in no time.

- With adequate carbohydrate content, you would always be filled with a constant energy.

- With a regulated blood sugar level, you can stay away from diseases like diabetes.

- There would be less anxiety and you would have a stable emotional level, which will make you think straight all the time.

- You will start drinking more water, which would keep you hydrated all day long.

- There will never be a scarcity of nutrients in your body after consuming just the right amount of vegetables and fruits.

- You will start appreciating your food more than ever. Not just its taste, its overall nutrient value will start turning you on.

- After a while, you would be able to distinguish between real hunger and emotional appetite.

- You will discover new cuisines and would taste some of the most delicious spices and vegetables in the process.

- You would spend more time cooking your meal, giving you a wide scope to experiment things in the kitchen.

- The strict plan will definitely boost your willpower. Since it is a 30-day challenge, you would definitely realize the power of self-control.

- As you would keep experimenting with different flavors, you will get a chance to reinvent yourself. You would gradually learn new things about yourself.

- Not just to reduce weight, the diet plan can also be implemented by those who would like to gain a healthy amount of weight.

- There is a huge Whole30 community online. You can be part of it and make new friends as well!

- You would get a chance to influence others and can even accompany someone else to take the Whole30 challenge again.

- You will get to learn new things about your body's metabolism and will gradually sync it all together.

- After a while, with the regular consumption of healthy food, enough water, getting regular sleep, you would have stronger hair and brighter skin.

- Needless to say, you would end up losing a lot of body fat.

- Your gym sessions would be more productive, resulting in the development of stronger muscles.

- You would feel more accomplished and satisfied.

- Most significantly, you would develop a healthy lifestyle that will soon become a habit in the most effortless way.

If all the above-listed reasons can't inspire you to try the revolutionary Whole30 diet plan, then nothing else can. It is quite addictive, as after successfully finishing the first 30-days, you would love to take another challenge for sure.

Yes, you might have to give up on some of your favorite food items during the process, but it would definitely be worth it. After completing the first cycle, you will feel a difference in your body.

After considering all these amazing benefits, Whole30 diet plan is something that should definitely be given a try. Let's move ahead and prepare yourself to commence this amazing process.

Chapter 3: How To Prepare For The Whole30 Diet Plan

Now when you are aware of some of the most striking benefits of the amazing Whole30 diet plan, you can definitely step it up and prepare yourself to commence this journey. As you already know that it is a 30-day challenge. In order to make sure that you complete it without facing any setback, make sure that you are all prepped up. Consider the following suggestions in mind and prepare yourself to take this amazing plan.

- Try to look for a partner: Even though you can take this challenge alone, it would always be nice to have someone by your side. If you already know someone who has completed the Whole30 diet, then ask for their assistance. Whenever you will crave for some junk food, you would have someone to talk to and can together come up with new cuisines.

- Come up with a plan: Just because you are undertaking a Whole30 diet plan, it doesn't mean that you have to stay at home and cook every meal, all by yourself. You can always plan your schedule and go out to consume selective meals. Always plan a day-wise schedule, so that you won't run out of meals.

- Be more creative: You can always come up with new and exciting ways to cook your food. Try to visit different aisles while shopping and experiment with various spices. It will definitely harness your cooking skills.

- Take time to prepare your meal: Initially, it would take a while for you to prepare every kind of meal. Since you would be avoiding ready-to-eat food, you might have to multitask a little and spend more time in the kitchen. It might seem a little overwhelming in the beginning, but you would get a hold of it in a few days. After a while, you would be a pro at it and would face no trouble to come up with a new meal instantaneously.

- Focus on a complete meal: Just because you are skipping a few things, it doesn't mean that you need to compromise with your overall eating habits. For instance, a lot of people think that Whole30 diet doesn't involve desserts. You can always prepare things like fruit salad, coconut flakes, grilled pineapples, cinnamon dishes, and more. Try to explore a little as there are plenty of alternatives out there to treat your sweet tooth.

- Set practical expectations: You need to understand that you can't lose 40 pounds in 30 days. Make sure that you dive in with a clear mindset. Don't think that it is a herculean task that can't be completed. There are thousands of people out there who have successfully completed the challenge. You can also be one of them.

- Don't slip: Until and unless you are starving and there is nothing healthy to eat around you, you can't just slip away and break the challenge. Whole30 diet plan requires a lot of willpower. It is a commitment in itself that you can't slip from for the next 30 days. You need to give the whole of you with 100% dedication. Instead of coming up with an excuse, try to make it work instead and be true to yourself.

- You can do this with a bit of effort: Truth to be told, it is not going to be a piece of cake. You have to learn how to say "No. Thank you!" to others. It would be a little challenging in the beginning, but after a while, when you'll see a visible change in your body, you would be inspired to bring a revolution in your life. With some resistance and perseverance, you can definitely excel in this challenge.

- Don't be obsessed: Try to be more natural and don't make the diet plan the core focus of your life. You should be more consistent and give an hour or two of every single day in order to work on your new diet plan. Don't weigh yourself every day. Do it after completing the entire challenge in order to get productive results. Be more serious and concerned about your health during the challenge. Every time you get tempted to try something else, restrain a little and remind yourself about your health.

- Be more diverse: Try to expand your horizon and educate yourself. To help you, we have introduced several dishes in this guide. This includes various healthy breakfast, lunch, and dinner recipes that are specifically designed for Whole30 diet plan. Try to prepare them and make sure that you follow your plan to attain productive results.

You can't complete this challenge without making a thoughtful schedule. When you make a daily schedule, keep the overall calorie and nutrient intake of your body in mind. Make sure that you don't compromise with your health and the overall need of your body while undertaking this process.

Now when you are well-equipped with all the resources, you can easily commence the Whole30 diet plan. We have carefully curated some of the healthiest recipes for you, so that you can complete the 30-day challenge without any setback. Move ahead and try these delicious recipes on your own.

Breakfast

Days: 1, 16

Sweet Potato & Apple Mesh
(Ready in 80 minutes with 10 minutes prep time- serves 2)

Ingredients:

- Protein of your choice

- I kg sweet potatoes (about 2 pounds)

- ¼ kilogram apples or applesauce (If buying from a shop check labels)

- Pinch of salt according to your preference

- Tablespoon ghee (optional)

- 3 tablespoons water

Cooking directions:

1. Before preheating oven to 400 degrees F. line the baking sheet with aluminum foil or parchment paper.

2. In the oven, roast sweet potatoes for 60 minutes then take out and cool.

3. While the sweet potatoes roast, make the applesauce by peeling and dicing the apples before cooking then

until soft. Once soft remove the lid and cook till all the water has evaporated.

4. After removing the skin from the sweet potatoes and apples, use a food processor to mesh the two to your desired texture.

5. Serve at your desired temperature.

Days: 2, 17

Breakfast Bacon Chicken Tenders & Apples

(Ready in 65 minutes with 10 minutes preparation time- serves 2)

Ingredients:

- 8 chicken tenders (boneless and skinless)

- 250 g bacon (check labels to ensure it is Whole30 compliant)

- Olive oil

Cooking directions:

1. Preheat oven to 375 degrees F.

2. Wrap separate chicken tenders in bacon.

3. Drizzle with olive oil once all the pieces are on the baking sheet.

4. Cook for 55 minutes in the oven. Ensure chicken is fully cooked and the bacon starts to be crisp.

5. Serve with vegetables of your choice or a green salad.

Days: 3, 18

Prosciutto-Wrapped Mango
(Ready in 8 minutes with 8 minutes preparation time)

Ingredients:

- 1 whole mango

- 1 packet mixed salad greens

- 1 package prosciutto (check packaging to ensure it is Whole30)

Cooking directions:

1. After peeling the mango, slice into thick spears along the length.

2. Wrap around each mango slices with prosciutto.

3. Serve above salad.

Days: 4, 19

Breakfast Meatcakes

(Ready in 45 minutes with 10 minutes preparation time- serves 4)

Ingredients:

- 1 teaspoon thyme

- 1 teaspoon rosemary

- 1 teaspoon cinnamon

- 1 tablespoon salt

- 1 teaspoon black pepper

- ½ teaspoon garlic powder

- ½ kg sugar-free sausage (ground)

- ½ kg chicken breast ground

- 14 strips of sugar-free bacon (nitrate)

- 1 apple (medium)

- 1/5 g blackberries

Cooking directions:

1. Preheat oven to 375 degrees

2. Prepare 14 cupcake pans.

3. Cut apples into small cubes.

4. Inside the cupcakes wrap the bacon on the walls of the cup, so it will hold the meat mixture.

5. Using your hands mash together the sausage, blackberries, apple. Zest, spices, and chicken.

6. Fill the cupcakes with the meat and spice mixture making sure that the bacon holds the mash inside.

7. Back in the oven for 35 minutes. Ensure that the bacon is fully cooked, if not use the broil function but keep watching.

8. Drain excess fat on the Meatcakes using paper towels.

Days: 5, 20

Bacon and Egg Sandwich with no Bread

(Ready in 30 minutes with 10 minutes preparation time- serves 2)

Ingredients:

- 4 slices bacon (check labels to ensure it is Whole30 compliant)

- 2 cups sliced mixed vegetables

- 3 eggs

- ½ tablespoon avocado oil

Cooking directions:

1. Use a nonstick pan to heat the oil.

2. Sauté the vegetables in the heated oil until soft. Make sure to sauté long enough that all excess water will be removed.

3. Cook the bacon in a separate pan.

4. Start by turning the heat to low on the vegetable pan for a few minutes then remove the pan altogether from the heat. Use the back of your cooking spoon to flatten the

vegetables while also moving them away from the edges of the pan towards the center of the pan.

5. After beating the eggs, add them to the vegetable pan spreading evenly on top of the vegetables but also making sure that the egg spread goes all the way to the edges of the pan and put back in the heat.

6. Once the bacon is done, remove from the pan, make sure to drain excess fat before you slice each piece in half and set aside.

7. Once the egg mixture stops bubbling, cover with a lid and continue cooking till the top is set nicely.

8. Remove from the pan soon as the eggs have set and put into a plate before you cut into quarters

9. Make the sandwich with the two-quarters and put the bacon inside.

Days: 6, 21

Broccoli Spinach Frittata

(Ready in 55 minutes with 10 minutes preparation time- serves 4)

Ingredients:

- 4 cups chopped broccoli florets

- 8 eggs

- 2 tablespoons ghee (You can use butter or coconut oil)

- ¼ teaspoon dried oregano

- 1 small onion (Cut into thin rings and then cut into half)

- ½ teaspoon unrefined sea salt

- 4 Cloves minced garlic

- 4 cups baby spinach (wash and cut roughly)

Cooking directions:

1. Preheat oven to 350 degrees F.

2. For 5 minutes steam broccoli till it starts to brown.

3. Using medium heat melt ghee in a big skillet the sauté the onion for between 20 and 25 minutes. (stir at intervals to prevent sticking)

4. After adding garlic sauté an extra two minutes.

5. Add the spinach and a pinch of salt then cook for 3 to 4 minutes.

6. Drain and rinse broccoli and add it in together with the oregano and the remainder of the sea salt and then stir well before removing from the heat.

7. At 350 degrees F, bake for 20 to 25 minutes until fully baked

8. Serve with avocado or any fermented vegetables you love.

Days: 7, 22

Spicy Chorizo Scotch Eggs
(Ready in 40 minutes with 10 minute's preparation time- serves 4)

Ingredients:

- 1/3 kg ground pork

- 1/3 kg chorizo

- 6 eggs, hardboiled

- 1 seeded and finely diced jalapeno

- ¼ cup chopped cilantro

- ½ teaspoon kosher salt

Cooking directions:

1. While you mix all the ingredients with your hands, preheat the oven to 375 degrees F.

2. Divide the mixture into six portions on top of a plastic sheet (separate for each piece) you lay on your working surface before you flatten each into a round shape of about half an inch thick.

3. Peel the hardboiled egg and put it in the center of each piece.

4. Use the plastic to fold the meat mixture around the egg.

5. Bake in 375 degrees inside a casserole dish for 30 minutes. Check to see if cooked properly otherwise, add some more time.

6. Serve at your desired temperature with a Whole30 compliant source.

Days: 8, 23

Sweet Potato Frittata
(Ready in 55 minutes with 10 minutes preparation time- serves 4)

Ingredients:

- ½ kg sweet potato

- ½ a bunch green onions

- 2 slices bacon

- 8 eggs

Cooking directions:

1. Preheat oven to 400 degrees F.

2. Over medium heat, in a skillet, cook bacon until crispy.

3. While bacon is cooking, slice the sweet potatoes along their length into four quarters. Cut each quarter into ¼" round shapes

4. As the bacon renders. Scoop a teaspoon of grease from the skillet and put into a pie pan and use it to coat the pan well.

5. Put the sweet potato slices into the pie pan and add several other spoons of the bacon grease over them and then cook the slices for 15 minutes inside the oven.

6. When sweet potatoes are cooked pour over them whipped eggs and put the pie pan back in the oven.

7. As the frittata is baking, take the bacon pieces off the skillet and drain on a paper towel and then once cooled cut into pieces.

8. Use the grease from the bacon to cook the green onions over low heat for a few minutes.

9. Once frittata has baked for 30 minutes and is now firm, take off from the oven and use the bacon pieces and wilted green onions as a topping. Serve warm.

Days: 9, 24

Dijon Pork Breakfast Skillet

(Ready in 30 minutes with 10 minutes preparation time- serves 5)

Ingredients:

- ½ kg ground pork

- 2 tablespoons Dijon Mustard (Check packaging for Whole30 compliance)

- ¼ kg mushrooms (Chop coarsely)

- ½ teaspoon basil

- ½ teaspoon salt

- ½ teaspoon garlic powder

- ½ teaspoon pepper

- 2 trimmed medium zucchini (cut into the shape of half moon)

- 1 tablespoon oil

Cooking directions:

1. Brown the mushrooms for 4 minutes in a large skillet with a heated tablespoon of oil.

2. Add the salt, pepper and the zucchini and cook for about 4 minutes or until tender.

3. Move vegetables to the fringes of the pan and leave space at the center open.

4. Into the middle space, add the ground pork and cook until brown. Take care not to mix the vegetables and the pork.

5. When pork is cooked, mix with the vegetables.

6. Add the Dijon and heat again before seasoning to taste.

Days: 10, 25

Baked Pears with Cranberries

(Ready in 40 minutes with 10 minutes preparation time- serves 4)

Ingredients:

- 2 pears (cut in half)

- 4 teaspoons coconut oil

- ½ an orange zested and juiced (divide in half)

- 1 cup cranberries

- Pinch cinnamon and nutmeg

Cooking directions:

1. Preheat oven to 350 degrees F.

2. Place the cut pears in a baking dish then sprinkle 1 teaspoon of coconut oil on each pear.

3. On each pear, add a pinch of nutmeg and cinnamon before adding the cranberries on top of and around the pears.

4. Over the pears and cranberries squeeze the orange juice.

5. Bake for about 30 minutes or till the pears soften and serve with a Whole30 compliant cream.

Days: 11, 26

Stuffed Tomatoes
(Ready in 40 minutes with preparation time of 10 minutes- serves 2)

Ingredients:

- 6 tomatoes

- ½ a dozen eggs

- 2 cups baby spinach

- Sea salt

Cooking directions:

1. Preheat oven to 390 degrees F.

2. Cut the tomato tops and the scoop out the insides using a spoon.

3. In a ceramic dish you have greased, place the tomatoes.

4. Fill the tomatoes with spinach, to ¾ full before sprinkling sea salt on the spinach.

5. Pour one egg over the spinach then bake for about 30 minutes. Check that the eggs are set.

6. Slightly sprinkle with pepper as you serve.

Days: 12, 27

Sweet Potato Breakfast Casserole
(Ready in 60 minutes with preparation time of 10 minutes- serves 4)

Ingredients:

For the sausage

- ½ a kg meat of your choice

- Black pepper (according to your preference)

- ½ teaspoon garlic powder

- ½ teaspoon sage

- 1 teaspoon salt

- ¼ teaspoon powdered thyme

- 1/8 teaspoon fennel

- Pinch red pepper flakes

Others

- 4 cups of sweet potatoes (peel and cube)

- Sea salt

- Freshly cracked pepper

- 1 diced onion

- ½ cup coconut milk

- 8 large or extra-large eggs

Cooking directions:

1. Combine all sausage ingredients in a skillet and cook until almost done before you add the onions and complete cooking.

2. While cooking, the sausage ingredients broil the sweet potatoes on high for 15 minutes stirring after 10 minutes.

3. Put oven at 350 degrees F.

4. Whisk eggs and coconut milk together before seasoning with salt and pepper.

5. In a 9 by 13-inch pan, spread the sweet potatoes and then spread the meat mixture on top before sprinkling with the bell peppers and pouring the eggs mixture on top of everything.

6. Bake for 30 minutes.

Days: 13, 28

Sausage and Egg Breakfast Bites
(Ready in 45 minutes with preparation time of 10 minutes- serves 4)

Ingredients:

- Small bunch of spinach (Use other dark greens available such as kale or beet greens)

- ½ cup crumbled sausage

- 10 eggs

- Small bunch of parsley (use other fresh herbs of your choice)

Cooking directions:

1. Preheat oven to 375 degrees F.

2. After slicing the greens into thin strips, sauté in oil on medium heat for about 5 minutes before adding the crumbled sausage.

3. Sauté till the sausage is properly cooked.

4. Whisk the eggs and then mix in the greens and cooked sausage.

5. Transfer into greased pan and bake for about 25 minutes.

6. Allow to cool a little before cutting into squares.

Days: 14, 29

Apple Berry Smoothie

(Ready in 12 minutes with preparation time of 10 minutes- serves 1)

Ingredients:

- ½ big apple

- 2 tablespoons flaked coconut (unsweetened)

- ½ a cup mixed frozen berries

- 1 egg

- Handful spinach

- 1 cup coconut milk

- 2 teaspoons coconut oil

- 1 Tablespoon chia seeds

Cooking directions:

1. Blend all ingredients in a blender.

Days: 15, 30

Sweet Potato Toast
(Ready in 45 minutes with 10 minutes prep time- serves 1)

Ingredients:

(Suit amounts to the number of people you want to serve)

- Sweet potato

Suggested toppings Toppings (pick any of your choices, check packages for processed food)

- Whole30 complying sausage

- Whole30 complying smoked salmon

- Pepper Slices

- Tomato slices

- Avocado slices

- Cucumber slices

Cooking directions:

1. Pre-heat oven to 400 degrees F.

2. Cut the sweet potato into uniform ¼ inch slices before coating each slice with oil and then sprinkling some salt slightly.

3. Cook for 20 minutes and the flip before cooking again for another 10 minutes.

4. After setting the oven to broil, cook each side again for about a minutes each till each slice is crisp.

5. Use your favorite ingredients to top up.

Lunch

Days: 1, 16

Loaded Guacamole Sweet Potato Fries

(Ready in 40 minutes with preparation time of 15 minutes- serves 4)

Ingredients:

- 2 large sweet potatoes

- 1 lime zest and juice

- 1 tablespoon chili powder

- 1 tablespoon olive oil

For Guacamole

- ½ a cup pico de gallo

- 1 large avocado

- ½ a cup sea salt (add more according to your preferences)

- 1 minced garlic clove

- 1/8 teaspoon cumin

- 3 chopped green onions

- 1 lime zest and juice

Cooking directions:

1. Preheat oven to 425 degrees F.

2. Cut sweet potatoes into chip size pieces before coating them with chili powder, olive oil and the zest and lime juice.

3. Roast in the oven for 30 minutes flipping over at halfway through the baking.

4. In a large bowl mash avocado then add garlic, lime and zest juice and the green onions before stirring to combine.

5. Move fries into a large plate them drizzle the guacamole on top.

6. Serve after sprinkling pico de gallo over.

Days: 2, 17

Ground Turkey Plantain Nachos
(Ready in 25 minutes with preparation time of 10 minutes- serves 2)

Ingredients:

- ½ kg organic lean ground turkey

- 2 cups shredded lettuce

- 2 tablespoons taco seasoning (check to see that it is Whole30 compliant)

- 170g plantain chips

- Toppings of your choice (consider peppers, guacamole, onions or tomatoes)

Cooking directions:

1. Brown ground turkey in a large skillet over medium heat for about 15 minutes or until it is not pink anymore.

2. Prepare your toppings at the same time as you brown the turkey.

3. Serve in this order: plantain chips at the bottom, your toppings and the ground turkey on top.

Days: 3, 18

Jalapeno Turkey Burgers
(Ready in 20 minutes with preparation time of 10 minutes- serves 4)

Ingredients:

- ½ kg ground turkey

- ½ tablespoon jalapeno pepper

- Pico de Gallo

- 1 medium peeled and minced the shallot.

- Guacamole

- 1 lime zest and juice

- ½ teaspoon black pepper

- ½ teaspoon sea salt

- 2 tablespoons chopped cilantro

- 1 teaspoon paprika

- 1 teaspoon cumin

Cooking directions:

1. Mix turkey, spices, herbs, and lime in a bowl using your hands.

2. Use the mixture to make four patties.

3. Add olive oil to pan placed on medium heat.

4. Place patties in a pan as soon as the oil is hot and cook for 5 minutes each side.

5. Serve topped with guacamole and Pico de Gallo (You can add egg if required)

Days: 4, 19

Whole30 Garlic Bacon Avocado Burgers

(Ready in 15 minutes with preparation time of 5 minutes- serves 7)

Ingredients:

- ¾ kilograms of ground beef

- 1 Avocado

- ¼ kg bacon (check ingredients to make sure it is Whole30 compliant)

- ¼ teaspoon cracked pepper (fresh)

- 6 large cloves garlic

- ¼ teaspoon sea salt

Cooking directions:

1. Ground the bacon strips (use a food processor, if you do not have one freeze the bacon and mince with a sharp knife).

2. Place crushed garlic in a bowl and then add the ground beef in, then sprinkle the salt and pepper over the meat.

3. Combine into a mixture using your hands.

4. Divide the mixture into patties of your preferable size.

5. In a heated skillet or frying pan cook each side for about 5 minutes over medium heat.

6. Serve with avocado slices

Cauliflower Rice Tabouleh

(Ready in 130 minutes with preparation time of 10 minutes- serves 4-6)

Ingredients:

- 1 head grated cauliflower rice

- ½ lemon

- 2 tablespoons olive oil

- 1 teaspoon chopped mint

- 1/3 cup chicken stock (check ingredients to ensure Whole30 compliance)

- 1 tablespoon chopped parsley

- 1 teaspoon sea salt

- ¼ cup finely chopped red onion

- 1 diced red pepper

- ½ a cup kalamata olives (cut them into halves)

Cooking directions:

1. Heat oil over medium-high heat in a large skillet and then add cauliflower rice, chicken stock, and salt before combining all.

2. Cook until soft and tender. Watch that it does not become soggy.

3. Take off from the heat and transfer to a bowl.

4. Remove additional moisture from cauliflower rice by continuing to toss.

5. Chill in refrigerator for two hours

6. When cooled sprinkle lemon juice, add red onion, mint, olives and parsley and toss.

7. Add salt and paper to taste and drizzle with olive oil before you serve.

Days: 6, 21

Zucchini & Sweet Potato Latkes
(Ready in 30 minutes with preparation time of 10 minutes- serves 2)

Ingredients:

- 1 cup shredded zucchini

- 1 tablespoon olive oil

- 1 cup shredded sweet potato

- 1 tablespoon ghee (You can also use clarified butter)

- 1 beaten egg

- Salt and pepper to taste

- I tablespoon coconut flour

- ½ a teaspoon dried parsley

- ½ teaspoon garlic powder

- ¼ teaspoon cumin

Cooking directions:

1. In a medium size bowl, mix the sweet potato, egg, and zucchini.

2. In a smaller bowl combine the spices, and coconut flour.

3. After dividing the mixture into four equal portions, drop into a heated non-stick pan that has ghee or olive oil. Press down with a cooking stock to make a ½ inch thick cake.

4. On medium heat, cook until golden brown before you flip and cook the other side.

5. Once cooked, remove from pan and drain extra oil on the cakes with paper towels.

6. Serve hot after seasoning with an additional sprinkle of kosher salt.

Days: 7, 22

Lemon Tahini Tuna Salad

(Ready in 15 minutes with preparation time of 15 minutes- serves 1)

Ingredients:

- 4 cups chopped mixed vegetables

- Sea salt and black pepper, to taste

- 1 Tablespoon tahini

- 1 can tuna or salmon in water

- 1 lemon juice

- ¼ teaspoon garlic powder

Cooking directions:

1. Arrange all the vegetables on a plate

2. In a medium bowl combine the tahini, garlic powder, and lemon juice.

3. Combine well by whisking (If it's too thick, add some water until you get to your desired thickness)

4. Add tuna to the dressing and mix gently. Add pepper and salt if you like.

5. Put the tuna mix on top of the prepared vegetables.

6. Serve chilled.

Days: 8, 23

Sweet Potato Sandwich

(Ready in 35 minutes with preparation time of 10 minutes- serves 2)

Ingredients:

- 4 slices of roasted chicken

- 1 large sweet potato (Thinly slice along the length)

- Guacamole

- Bacon (check packaging to ensure it is Whole30 compliant)

- Lettuce

- Tomato

- Salt and pepper

Cooking directions:

1. Preheat oven to 400 degrees F.

2. Lightly grease baking sheet before you place seasoned sweet potatoes.

3. Bake for about 12 minutes for each side or watch for a golden brown color.

4. Assemble the sandwich by putting all the ingredients in-between two layers of roasted sweet potatoes.

Days: 9, 24

Sheet Pan Fajitas

(Ready in 35 minutes with preparation time of 10 minutes- serves 4-6)

Ingredients:

- ½ a kg thinly sliced chicken breasts

- ½ teaspoon ground pepper

- 1 teaspoon salt

- 1 Sliced yellow pepper

- 1 sliced green pepper

- 1 sliced red pepper

- Pinch chili flakes

- 1 halved onion cut into slices

- ½ teaspoon garlic powder

- ¼ cup olive oil

- 2 teaspoons chili powder

- 1 teaspoon cumin

Cooking directions:

1. Preheat oven to 400 degrees F.

2. Combine garlic, oil, chili flakes, chili powder, cumin, salt and pepper in a small bowl.

3. In a large sheet pan, toss the mixture you made above, the chicken and vegetables and spread evenly.

4. Bake for about 30 minutes. Check that the chicken is cooked and the vegetables are soft and crispy.

5. Serve with avocado or sour cream.

Days: 10, 25

Gluten Free Meatballs with Vegetables and Herbs

(Ready in 40 minutes with preparation time of 10 minutes- serves 4)

Ingredients:

- ½ Kg ground beef or lamb

- 1 egg

- ¼ cup grated cauliflower

- 1/8 cup carrots juice (You can use carrot pulp)

- 1 tablespoon dried onion flakes (Can be replaced with 3 tablespoons of fresh minced onion)

- 1 teaspoon fish source (Additive free)

- 2 tablespoons finely chopped fresh herbs (Can replace this with 1 tablespoon dried herbs)

- Sea salt

Cooking directions:

1. Preheat oven to 400 degrees F.

2. Mix the egg, garlic, onion, meat, and vegetables with your hands in a bowl until you have a mixture that is even and smooth.

3. After mixing the herbs, fish sauce and salt with the meat mixture roll into meatballs 2-inch each.

4. On a baking sheet, bake for 30 minutes. Make sure the meatballs are well cooked to a brown color.

5. Serve at your desired temperature.

Days: 11, 26

Green Fajita Chicken

(Ready in 60 minutes with preparation time of 40 minutes- serves 6-8)

Ingredients:

- 1 kg chicken breasts (Cut into strips)

- Fresh cilantro to taste

- 2 deseeded jalapenos

- 1 lime juice

- ¼ avocado oil

- ¼ teaspoon ground cumin

- 6 cloves peeled garlic

Cooking directions:

1. Slice chicken into long thin pieces

2. Chop jalapeno into cubes and peel the garlic before adding all the other ingredients except the chicken in a blender and liquefy. Thin with water if you think the marinade is too thick.

3. Add the marinade into a baggie with the chicken and coat the chicken evenly and put in the fridge for 30 minutes.

4. In a large skillet with some extra coconut oil brown the chicken evenly, takes about 8 to 10 minutes. Flip chicken once one side is browned and brown the other (For this recipe split into two batches of half the ingredients to cook all at once).

5. Once the chicken is thoroughly cooked remove from the heat and prepare to serve.

Days: 12, 27

"Spaghetti" with Beef Sauce

(Ready in 30 minutes with preparation time of 10 minutes- serves 6)

Ingredients:

- 2 diced tomatoes with garlic and basil

- 2 tablespoons Sausage seasoning (Check labels to see that it is Whole30 Compliant).

- ¾ of a kg ground beef (Grass fed)

- 5 tablespoons Tomato Paste

- 6 medium Zucchini

- 1 tablespoon sea salt

- ¼ cup Extra Virgin olive oil

- ½ teaspoon Black Pepper

- ½ a teaspoon dried oregano

- 1 teaspoon dried basil

- 1 garlic clove

Cooking directions:

1. Blend the tomatoes and the oregano on high until you have a smooth texture.

2. Over medium heat, warm the sauce in olive oil.

3. Make the "noodles" then add to the sauce to make soft.

4. Brown the beef and seasoning mixture in a skillet over medium-high heat.

5. Add to the sauce.

6. Cook until properly heated and the "noodles" are soft.

7. Serve at your desired temperature.

Days: 13, 28

Italian Turkey Chili

(Ready in 25 minutes with preparation time of 15 minutes- serves 8)

Ingredients:

- 1 kg ground turkey thigh

- ¾ of a liter prepared red sauce

- ½ kg frozen chopped spinach

- 2 tablespoons Italian sausage seasoning

Cooking directions:

1. Combine chopped spinach, turkey thigh, and Italian sausage seasoning in a large pot.

2. Over medium heat cook until the turkey is cooked and the spinach is fully wilted. This can take about 10 minutes. Turn periodically to prevent parts remaining undercooked. If there is excess liquid, do not drain.

3. After adding read source, heat for another 5 minutes.

4. Simmer on low heat until you are ready to serve.

Days: 14, 29

Simple Shrimp Ceviche

(Ready in 375 minutes with preparation time of 15 minutes- serves 3)

Ingredients:

- ¼ kg raw shrimp

- Salt and pepper

- 1 diced large tomato

- ¼ cup chopped cilantro

- 1 minced garlic clove

- Juice from two lemons

- ½ an avocado

- Juice from 1 orange

- ½ minced jalapeno pepper (Optional)

Cooking directions:

1. After peeling the shrimp, chop into small pieces.

2. Prepare the vegetables by dicing the tomato, mincing the jalapeno and garlic, and cubing the avocado.

3. In a bowl, mix the avocado, shrimp, garlic, tomato, and jalapeno with the citrus juice. Make sure you have enough liquid to adequately cover the shrimp.

4. Refrigerate for 6 hours. Watch for the shrimp to turn to opaque from the original translucent.

5. Before serving, adjust seasoning with salt and pepper according to your taste and top with cilantro.

Days: 15, 30

Chicken with Rosemary & Roasted Oranges

(Ready in 50 minutes with preparation time of 15 minutes- serves 6)

Ingredients:

- 6 whole chicken legs (about 1 ½ kg.)

- Salt and pepper

- 2 large oranges

- 2 springs of fresh rosemary (Remove leaves from stems and chop finely)

- 2 teaspoons garlic powder

Cooking directions:

1. Preheat oven to 400 degrees F.

2. After zesting the orange set aside. Into a small bowl, mix together the orange zest, fresh rosemary, and dried garlic and set aside as you prepare the chicken.

3. On a lined baking tray, lay the chicken legs. (Remove the chicken skin from the leg but still leave attached to the base of the drumstick.

4. Press the orange zest on the chicken legs so that when you return the skin the zest is between the skin and the leg. Add the salt and pepper at this moment.

5. Remove the remaining skin on the oranges and cut the orange into quarters. Around the chicken pieces in the baking tray, lay the oranges.

6. Roast in the oven till chicken is properly cooked. The edges of the orange slices should also be starting to caramelize. This should take about 35 minutes.

7. Set aside for at least 10 minutes before you serve.

Dinner

Day: 1

Thai Chicken with Spicy Peanut Sauce

(Ready in 25 minutes with preparation time of 10 minutes- serves 3-4)

Ingredients:

- 2 thinly sliced sweet peppers

- 1 date

- Water

- Chopped Cilantro

- Sesame seeds

- 1 pressed garlic clove

- 1 handful carrot shreds

- 1 tablespoon finely grated fresh ginger

- 2 medium spiralized zucchinis

- ¼ cup sunflower butter

- Salt

- Pepper

- Juice of ½ lime

- ½ a kg chicken tenders

- 4 tablespoons coconut aminos

- 1 Tablespoon sesame oil

- 1/8 tablespoon salt

- 4 tablespoons olive oil

- Red pepper flakes

Cooking directions:

1. In a small cup cover the date with water and microwave for one minute on high and leave to soak.

2. Whisk together salt, garlic, sesame oil, ginger, coconut aminos, sunflower butter, and lemon juice in a small bowl.

3. After removing date from water, cut the pit out and discard and then smash the date into a paste and add to the rest of the peanut sauce and then add a dash of fresh pepper according to your preferences.

4. After warming 2 tablespoons of olive oil in a skillet at medium-high heat add the chicken pieces. Sauté each side for 4 minutes and then remove the chicken from skillet and put aside.

5. Add the remaining 2 tablespoons of olive oil into the same skillet and toss the sweet peppers, zucchini and

carrot shreds. Cook for 2 minutes constantly stirring to soften the vegetables.

6. Once chicken is diced and tossed with the veggie noodles, stir the sauce in before you serve.

7. For garnishing, use sesame seeds and cilantro.

Day: 2

Lemon Chicken & Potatoes

(Ready in 75 minutes with preparation time of 15 minutes- serves 4-6)

Ingredients:

- 8-10 pieces of chicken (Leave skin on)

- ½ a teaspoon fresh ground pepper

- ½ kg baby red potatoes

- 1 ½ teaspoons salt

- ½ onion (cut into large pieces)

- ½ teaspoon crushed red pepper flakes

- 1 Juiced lemon

- 1 Sliced onion

- 1 tablespoon fresh rosemary, springs for garnish.

- 2 minced garlic cloves

Cooking directions:

1. Preheat oven to 400 degrees F.

2. On a glass baking dish sprayed with baking spray arrange the chicken pieces making sure that the skin side is up, lemon slices, potatoes, and the onion.

3. Whisk together the salt, pepper, lemon juice, crushed red pepper flakes, olive oil, rosemary, and garlic. Over the chicken and potatoes in the pan, pour the mixture and sprinkle additional salt and pepper over.

4. Bake for an hour, uncovered. Make sure the potatoes and chicken are fully cooked.

Day: 3

Grilled Salmon with Mango Salsa
(Ready in 25 minutes with preparation time of 10 minutes- serves 4)

Ingredients:

- 4 175 g salmon fillets

- Juice of 1 lime

- 1 teaspoon garlic powder

- Salt and pepper to taste

- 1 teaspoon chili powder

Mango salsa

- 3 diced mangos

- ¼ cup roughly chopped packed cilantro leaves

- ½ cup diced red pepper

- 1 small seeded and finely chopped jalapeno

- 1 diced red onion

Cooking directions:

1. Stir together the cilantro, mangos, jalapenos, red peppers, and onions and then set aside.

2. Create a mixture of salt and pepper, garlic powder and chili powder and use to smear into the salmon fillets.

3. Over medium heat, grill the fillets for 7 minutes on each side.

4. Over the grilled salmon, squeeze fresh lime juice.

5. Before serving, top with Salsa.

Day: 4

Shrimp and Asparagus Stir-Fry
(Ready in 15 minutes with preparation time of 5 minutes- serves 4)

Ingredients:

- 2 tablespoons coconut oil

- 2/3 cup broth

- 1 pound peeled shrimp

- ½ teaspoon ground ginger

- 1 bundle chopped asparagus

- 4 cloves minced garlic

- 2 tablespoons lemon juice

Cooking directions:

1. Over medium heat, heat the coconut oil in a skillet pan

2. Into the pan add the ginger, shrimp, garlic, and asparagus and cook for 2 minutes before stirring and cooking for another 5 minutes.

3. After adding the broth, simmer for another 2 to 4 minutes until the asparagus is tender and serve.

Day: 5

Skillet Beef Fajitas

(Ready in 32 minutes with preparation time of 10 minutes- serves 3)

Ingredients:

Steak

- ¾ kg flank steak (sliced into ribbons along the grain)
- ¼ teaspoon ground black pepper
- 1 lime juice
- ½ a teaspoon sea salt
- ½ teaspoon chili powder
- ½ teaspoon dried oregano
- ¼ teaspoon ground cayenne red pepper
- 1/8 teaspoon ground black pepper
- 1/8 teaspoon paprika
- 1/8 teaspoon cumin

Vegetables

- 2 tablespoons organic coconut oil
- 1 thinly sliced avocado, seeded.

- 1 yellow bell pepper, de-seeded, trimmed and sliced

- 1 red pepper, de-seeded, trimmed and sliced

- ¼ cup chopped cilantro

- 1 minced garlic clove

- 1 thinly sliced jalapeno (Remove seeds if you do not want it to be too hot)

- 150g shitake mushrooms

- 1 cup vegetable broth

- 2 sliced green onions

Cooking directions:

1. Coat steak with lime juice and spices in a large bowl and set aside.

2. Lay the steak in single layers in a heavy skillet with heated coconut oil over medium heat.

3. For 4 minutes per side, allow the steak to sear, then remove from pan and set aside on a plate.

4. Use the juice from the steak to toss onions, pepper, garlic and mushrooms in the pan until they are soft, this should take about 5 minutes.

5. Add the vegetable broth, green onions, jalapeno, steak and any juices collecting on the plate.

6. After tossing, cook for another 7 minutes.

7. After removing from heat and tossing again, throw the cilantro on top and the sliced avocados.

8. Serve with tortillas or lettuce cups.

Day: 6

<u>Pork Roast with Sweet Potatoes, Apples, and Onions</u>

(Ready in 55 minutes with preparation time of 10 minutes- serves 3)

Ingredients:

- 1 kg pork roast (tie to help hold shape)

- ¼ cup olive oil (You can add more if not enough to coat)

- Salt and pepper

- Salt and pepper to taste

- 4 quartered apples (use 2 if apples are large)

- ¼ teaspoon chili powder

- 2 sweet potatoes, cut into wedges

- ½ teaspoon sweet paprika

- 1 sweet onion sliced

Cooking directions:

1. Preheat broiler to 500 degrees F.

2. After rubbing pork with olive oil, season with salt and pepper.

3. Broil for 15 minutes on a sheet tray. Flip at the half way point so that you get a uniform color on the meat.

4. While the meat cooks, chop the onions, apples, and sweet potatoes before tossing in the oil and spices and then arrange around the pork in the sheet tray.

5. After turning down the heat to 450 degrees F (at this point turn the oven setting back to conventional). Roast for 20 to 30 minutes. Make sure that the sweet potatoes and apples are tender.

6. Let the meat rest for 10 minutes before you slice it.

7. Put back sliced pork and juices to the pan

8. Serve with onions, apples, sweet potatoes, onions and a Whole30 compliant salad.

Day: 7

<u>Marinated Steak with Roasted Red Pepper Pesto</u>

(Ready in 40 minutes with preparation time of 30 minutes- serves 3)

Ingredients:

- ½ kg steak

- 1 teaspoon onion powder

- ¼ cup balsamic vinegar

- 1 teaspoon salt

- 2 tablespoons avocado or olive oil

- 1 teaspoon pepper

- ¼ cup chopped fresh basil or 1 tablespoon dried basil

- 1 tablespoon fresh minced garlic or 1 teaspoon garlic powder

- 1 teaspoon pepper

Roasted Red Pepper Pesto

- ½ cup fresh basil

- ½ teaspoon pepper

- ½ cup roasted peppers

- ½ teaspoon salt ¼ cup pine nuts

- 1 large garlic clove

- ¼ cup olive oil

Cooking directions:

1. Marinate steak overnight in a plastic bag. If there is not time marinate for at least 4 hours.

2. Sear steak in ghee or grill to your preferred level.

3. Prepare pesto while the steak is cooking by adding all the pesto ingredients into a food processor and combining in a pesto texture.

4. Serve steak with pesto on top.

Day: 8

Carne Asada

(Ready in 30 minutes with preparation time of 20 minutes- serves 4)

Ingredients:

- 1 1/3 kg flank or skirt steak (each should be 1 inch thick)

- 1 teaspoon smoked paprika

- 1/3 cup white vinegar

- 1 teaspoon dried oregano

- 1/3 cup olive oil

- 1 teaspoon cumin

- 2 juiced limes

- 4 cloves minced garlic

- 1 teaspoon garlic powder

- 1 teaspoon salt

- 1 teaspoon chili powder

- 1 teaspoon pepper

Cooking directions:

1. In a bowl, combine together the spices, white vinegar, olive oil, garlic, and line lime juice and mix well.

2. Coat the steak with the marinade and keep in the fridge at least an hour. If time permits 24 hours.

3. In an oven turned to broil, place the steak in baking sheet and have the rack sitting in the top position. Broil steak for 10 minutes flipping half way through. You can cook longer if you want the steak to be well done. The more you cook the steak, the more it gets tough.

4. After resting for 10 minutes, cut the steak into slices before serving with salsa, fresh cilantro, and lime wedges.

Day: 9

Crockpot Balsamic Roast Beef

(Ready in 490 minutes with preparation time of 10 minutes- serves 6)

Ingredients:

- 2 kg roast

- Sea salt and pepper to taste (put according to your preferences)

- 1 diced medium onion

- 2 pinches of red pepper flakes

- 6 cloves minced garlic

- ½ cup balsamic vinegar

- 1 cup beef stock

- 2 tablespoons coconut aminos

Cooking directions:

1. With the fat side down, put the whole roast in crockpot.

2. Over the top of the roast, add in the remaining ingredients and then add the salt and pepper over the

top. Save some onion and garlic to use for your gravy.

3. Cover the pot and cook on low for 8 hours. The meat is cooked when it turns brown and starts to shred very easily.

4. Take the roast off the crockpot.

5. Make gravy by blending (with an immersion blender) the juices that remain in the crockpot with onion and garlic until the desired consistency is reached.

6. Serve roast beef with gravy.

Day: 10

Salmon and Avocado Salsa

(Ready in 25 minutes with preparation time of 15 minutes- serves 4-6)

Ingredients:

- 1 kg salmon

- 2 tablespoons of avocado oil (use any oil that is Whole30 compliant)

- 1 teaspoon cumin

- 1 teaspoon onion powder

- 1 teaspoon smoked paprika

- Salt and pepper to taste

For the Avocado Salsa

- 2 peeled and diced avocados

- 2 tablespoons chopped fresh cilantro

- 1 finely diced small red onion

- 1 small red onion

- 2 tablespoons olive oil

- 3 seeded and finely diced peppers

- Juice of 3 limes

- Salt and pepper to taste

Cooking directions:

1. In a bowl, combine all the salsa ingredients and place in the fridge.

2. Preheat oven to 400 degrees F.

3. In a lightly greased baking pan, place the salmon.

4. In a small bowl, combine the spices and then rub the mixture on each side of the salmon.

5. Over each piece of salmon, place a pat of butter and bake for 12 to 15 minutes or watch for salmon to start flaking easily with a fork.

6. Serve salmon with avocado salsa.

Day: 11

Greek Meatballs with Avocado Tzatziki Sauce

(Ready in 35 minutes with preparation time of 10 minutes- serves 6)

Ingredients:

For Greek meatballs

- ½ kg ground lamb (you can also use beef)

- ½ teaspoon ground cumin

- ½ cup of finely diced red onion

- 1 teaspoon ground coriander.

- 2 cloves minced garlic

- 1 tablespoon chopped fresh oregano (1 teaspoon dried oregano)

- Zest of half lemon

- Sea salt and pepper to taste

Avocado Tzatziki

- 1 avocado

- 1 teaspoon fresh dill (you can use mint if you prefer)

- 1 small cucumber cut into half and seeds removed

- 2 cloves garlic

- Juice of 1 lemon

- 1 tablespoon diced red onion

- Sea salt and pepper to taste

Cooking directions:

1. Preheat oven to 350 degrees F.

2. Make the meatballs (about 2 inches each) by combining all the meatball ingredients.

3. Bake for 25 minutes on a raised edge baking pan.

4. Serve the meatballs with avocado Tzatziki sauce.

Avocado Tzatziki sauce

1. Blend all the Avocado Tzatziki ingredients in a food blender to a smooth and creamy texture.

Day: 12

Salmon Balls

(Ready in 30 minutes with preparation time of 10 minutes- serves 3)

Ingredients:

- 350g canned salmon

- 1 tablespoon olive oil for greasing (You can use avocado or coconut oil)

- ¼ cup finely diced red onion

- 1 tablespoon chopped fresh dill or basil

- 1 egg

- 1 tablespoon chopped green onion

- ½ lemon. Zested and juiced

- Sea salt and pepper to taste.

Cooking directions:

1. Preheat oven to 350 degrees F.

2. In a bowl, mix well all the ingredients, except the oil, and then use the mixture to make the salmon balls.

3. Pour oil into a baking pan and place the salmon balls in it. Roll the balls in fat before you start baking.

4. Bake for 20 minutes and serve.

Day: 13

Sriracha Lime Chicken Skillet

(Ready in 90 minutes with preparation time of 60 minutes- serves 4)

Ingredients:

- 6 boneless chicken thighs

- Cilantro for garnish

- Salt and pepper

- 1 tablespoon Sriracha (Make your own, the one from the store is not Whole30 compliant)

- ¼ cup extra virgin olive oil

- ½ sliced large onion

- Juice of 1 lime

Cooking directions:

1. After washing and patting chicken dry, season with salt and pepper.

2. Combine the chicken, olive oil, onion slices, lime juice, and sriracha, in a large bowl then toss to coat. Place inside the refrigerator for an hour.

3. Preheat the oven to 400 degrees F.

4. In a large ovenproof skillet, place the chicken and pour on top of the chicken, the onion/marinade mixture.

5. Bake for 25 minutes before broiling for another 5, the chicken will start to brown and look crisp.

6. After removing from the oven, garnish with cilantro.

Day: 14

Pulled Tandoori Chicken

(Ready in 27 minutes with preparation time of 10 minutes- serves 4)

Ingredients:

For the chicken

- 1 kg chicken breasts (trim the fat and cut into portions the size of a palm)

- 2 cloves minced garlic

- 4 cups chicken stock

- ½ finely chopped onion

- Pinch of sea salt

For Tandoori sauce

- ½ cup full-fat coconut milk

- 1 teaspoon black pepper

- 1 teaspoon sea salt

- 1 teaspoon turmeric

- 1 teaspoon smoked paprika

- 1 teaspoon cayenne pepper (optional)

Cooking directions:

Chicken

1. In a large pot, fill in the chicken stock then add onion and garlic and get to boil.

2. When it starts to boil, add the chicken and then after 2 minutes reduce the heat to low and leave to simmer for 12 to 15 minutes. The chicken should be fully cooked and not be pink anymore. Take away from the heat and immediately drain and leave to cool.

3. Once the chicken is cool, shred finely.

4. Serve immediately after adding the tandoori sauce.

Tandoori sauce

1. All the spices should be combined in a small bowl and coconut milk added.

Day: 15

Turkey Sweet Potato

(Ready in 25 minutes with preparation time of 5 minutes- serves 3)

Ingredients:

- ½ kg lean ground turkey

- 2 strips diced bacon

- 1 cup cooked mashed sweet potato

- ½ a cup diced onion

- 1 egg

- 2 jalapenos

- 2 cloves minced garlic

- ½ cup diced onion

Cooking directions:

1. In a large bowl, combine all the ingredients.

2. After mixing well, form into meatballs.

3. At 400 degree F. bakes for 18 to 20 minutes. Flip once at Midway. (Can be cooked in a pan if your prefer)

Day: 16

Grilled BBQ Short Ribs

(Ready in 105 minutes with preparation time of 45 minutes- serves 4)

Ingredients:

For the ribs

- 2 ¼ kg short ribs

- 1/3 teaspoon onion powder

- 1 tablespoon coconut sugar

- 1 teaspoon kosher salt

- 1 teaspoon smoked paprika

- 1 teaspoon garlic powder

- BBQ sauce

For the pineapple

- 3 large fresh pineapple rings

- Splash rice vinegar

- 1/3 cup chopped red bell pepper

- ¼ cup chopped cilantro leaves

- 1 teaspoon minced jalapeno

- Splash rice vinegar

Cooking directions:

1. Remove as much fat as you can from the ribs and set it aside.

2. In a small bowl, mix the spices and the coconut sugar.

3. After covering each short rib with the mixture allow to sit aside for about an hour.

4. Preheat outdoor grill to 400 degrees F. leave one of the burners off so that you can use it later to cook the ribs in indirect heat.

5. Cut enough aluminum foil to cover the ribs. Before covering each rib in the foil, put 2 ice cubes on both sides of the rib and fold the aluminum foil over. Leave a little space for air to escape while cooking.

6. Cook over indirect heat for 2 hours or until tender.

7. Set aside for a few minutes after removing from the grill.

For pineapple salsa

1. While cooking the ribs, place pineapple rings on the grill and cook for about 5 minutes per side. The pineapple should start to caramelize.

2. Chop after removing from grill.

3. Toss pineapple in a bowl with the remaining ingredients.

4. Serve together with the short ribs.

Day: 17

Beef and Root Vegetable Stew

(Ready in 70 minutes with preparation time of 10 minutes- serves 6 to 8)

Ingredients:

- 2 pounds beef stew meat

- 3 carrots, peeled and chopped

- 1 large yellow onion, chopped into wedges

- 4 cloves garlic, minced

- 3 stalks celery, chopped

- 1 large navel orange, chopped into eighths

- 3 sprigs thyme

- 1 bay leaf

- 1 cinnamon stick

- 2 cups beef broth

- 1 16-ounce can tomato paste

- 1 teaspoon kosher salt

- 1 large yucca root, cooked

- 1.5 cups frozen peas

Cooking directions:

1. Add all the ingredients except the tomato paste, kosher salt, yucca root and frozen peas, into a large stock pot and refrigerate for 12 to 24 hours.

2. Prepare the yucca root and keep in the refrigerator.

3. When ready to cook, take out the cinnamon stick from the pot and get the ingredients in the pot to boil over medium heat.

4. Add the tomato paste together with the salt and reduce the heat to allow to simmer. Cook until all the vegetables have softened and the meat is properly cooked.

5. When the meat is cooked, add the frozen peas and yucca root and simmer for another 15 minutes.

6. Take out the oranges, thyme and bay leaf from the stew before serving with your mashed sweet potatoes.

Day: 18

Apricot Ginger Glazed Pork Chops

(Ready in 25 minutes with preparation time of 10 minutes- serves 4)

Ingredients:

- 1 ½ teaspoons kosher salt

- 2/3 apricot preserves (If you can't find then, use apricot pineapple preserves)

- 1 teaspoon garlic powder

- ½ cup chicken broth

- 1 teaspoon onion powder

- 1 teaspoon ginger powder

- ½ teaspoon pepper

- 1 clove minced garlic (use ½ teaspoon if jarred)

- 4 boneless pork chops

- 2 tablespoons olive oil (1 for coating)

Cooking directions:

1. Over medium-high heat, heat a large skillet with olive oil.

2. In the meanwhile, mix the pepper, salt, onion and garlic, and then dip one side of the pork lightly in the mixture.

3. Once the olive oil is hot put the pork into the pan with the spiced side facing down. On top of the pork chops, sprinkle the spice mixture left over.

4. Cook for about 3 minutes before you flip over and then cook for another 3 minutes.

5. Take the pork off the pan and cover with foil to keep warm.

6. Reduce heat and then add the other tablespoon of olive oil, garlic, and ginger and sauté for 30 minutes while steering.

7. Add the chicken broth and allow to simmer. Keep scraping the browned bits that accumulate at the bottom of the pan while simmering for an extra 1 minute.

8. After whisking in the preserves, simmer the sauce and then add back the pork to your pan and cook for another three minutes per side.

9. Allow to rest for 5 minutes before you serve.

Day: 19

Crock Pot Boneless Pork

(Ready in 370 minutes with preparation time of 10 minutes- serves 4-6)

Ingredients:

- 1 kg pork roast (boneless)

- 1 cup apple cider (with no artificial sweetening)

- 2 teaspoons sea salt

- Loose leaf tea

- 4 minced cloves large garlic

- 1 ½ cups boiling water

Cooking directions:

1. Sprinkle both sides of the pork roast with kosher salt and then pat gentle the minced garlic into the pork.

2. In 1 ½ cups of boiling water in a mug, put in the loose leaf tea and leave to steep for a period of 8 minutes, then add to the crockpot together with the apple cider.

3. After adding in the pork roast on top of the liquid set the crock pot on low and cook for 6 hours. Get some liquid from the pot on the meat periodically as it cooks.

4. When the meat is cooked, remove from the pot and cut off the netting.

5. Shred the meat on a cutting board before putting it back in the crock pot that has the juices and cooking for another 10 minutes.

Day: 20

Pork Ragu

(Ready in 485 minutes with preparation time of 5 minutes- serves 12)

Ingredients:

- 1 diced onion

- 2 tablespoons fresh thyme leaves

- 3 diced small carrots

- 1 teaspoon crushed hot red pepper flakes

- 3 thinly sliced cloves garlic

- 1 ½ liter diced tomatoes

- 2 springs fresh thyme

- 1.8 kg pork shoulder

- Kosher salt and freshly ground pepper to taste

Cooking directions:

1. Use the thyme, onions, garlic and carrots to make a nest in the slow cooker dish and then add the pork on top before pouring in the diced tomatoes.

2. Cook for 8 hours on high.

3. Once cooked, break the pork apart and throw away any parts of fat that have not been thoroughly cooked and the thyme wood too.

4. Before serving, season with the black pepper, thyme, hot pepper flakes and kosher salt.

Day: 21

Whole30 Meatloaf

(Ready in 78 minutes with preparation time of 8 minutes- serves 4)

Ingredients:

- 1/2 kg ground turkey (You can use beef)

- 4 pressed large garlic cloves

- 1 diced bell pepper

- 2 eggs

- ½ medium sized diced yellow onion

- ½ cup Whole30 Ketchup

Cooking directions:

1. Preheat oven to 350 degrees F.

2. Mix all the ingredients thoroughly in a large bowl using your hands, including the egg without the crust.

3. Put into an ungreased loaf pan measuring 9" by 5".

4. Pack the mixed ingredients down but leave space on the edges of the pan so that the grease produced while you cook will collect.

5. Bake in the oven on the center rack for 1 hour 10 minutes before you serve.

Day: 22

Simple Shrimp Ceviche

(Ready in 50 minutes with preparation time of 5 minutes- serves 5)

Ingredients:

- 2 chicken breasts (cut in half)
- ½ cup vegetable broth
- 6 chicken drumsticks
- 150 g frozen spinach
- 2 tablespoons extra-virgin oil
- 1 handful sun-dried tomatoes packed in oil.
- Sea salt and pepper
- 400 g artichoke hearts (drain and cut into quarters)
- 1 sliced medium lemon
- 3 sliced carrots

Cooking directions:

1. Preheat oven to 425 degrees F.
2. With salt and pepper, season the chicken generously.

3. In an oven-proof skillet heat the oil.

4. Brown the chicken on all sides in the oil.

5. Remove chicken and keep on a plate.

6. Add artichoke hearts, onions, sun-dried tomatoes and carrots and sauté to get the vegetable to soften a little.

7. Add the spinach and broth and then stir until the spinach starts to wilt.

8. Put the chicken back in the pan with the vegetables.

9. With the pan back in the oven, roast until the chicken is fully cooked.

10. Place hot skillet on a trivet on top of the table as soon as you remove from the oven.

Day: 23

<u>Avocado Cups with Bacon & Egg Salad</u>

(Ready in 12 minutes with preparation time of 5 minutes- serves 3)

Ingredients:

- 6 Pastured eggs

- Organic red cayenne pepper (optional)

- 6 slices pastured bacon

- 3 organic avocados

- 1 tablespoon plain yogurt (ensure it is Whole30 compliant)

- Organic black pepper to taste

- Real salt to taste

- 2 organic sliced green onions

Cooking directions:

1. As you hard-boil the eggs in a saucepan, cook the bacon until it's at the crispness level you desire.

2. Remove eggshells. (To make peeling process easier keep them in cold water for about a minute)

3. With the plain yogurt, mash the eggs in a bowl and season with salt and pepper, then crumble the bacon in.

4. Remove the pit from the avocado you have cut into half.

5. Full the avocados with the eggs salad mixture and on top sprinkle with red cayenne pepper.

Day: 24

<u>Creamy Su-Dried Tomato Chicken</u>
(Ready in 17 minutes with preparation time of 5 minutes- serves 4)

Ingredients:

- Chicken breasts (You can use whole or cut into strips)

- Sea salt and black pepper to taste

- Coconut cream

- Arrowroot powder

- Sun dried tomatoes (Remember to drain if packed in oil)

- Olive oil

- Chicken broth

- Minced garlic

- Chopped fresh basil

Cooking directions:

1. With the sea salt and pepper, season all the sides of the chicken breasts.

2. Over medium heat, heat the olive oil in a large skillet and then add the chicken breasts. Sear to a golden color on all the sides and remove from pan (Keep warm by covering with foil).

3. In the meantime, whisk the arrowroot into a consistent mixture with the chicken broth.

4. After adding the garlic to the skillet, continue cooking for another 30 seconds and then add the broth/arrowroot mixture, half of the fresh basil, coconut cream, and sun dried tomatoes.

5. Bring the heat down and simmer the sauce till it thickens, takes about 3 minutes and then season with black pepper and sea salt.

6. Put the chicken back into the pan and scoop some sauce over it and cook for another minute.

7. Before serving, sprinkle the remaining fresh basil on top of the chicken.

Rustic Chorizo Pasta

(Ready in 20 minutes with preparation time of 10 minutes- serves 3)

Ingredients:

- 1.2 kg chorizo

- ½ diced sweet onion

- Fresh parsley for garnish (optional)

- 2 peeled and spiralized zucchinis

- 400 grams diced tomatoes

- ½ teaspoon pepper

- ½ teaspoon sea salt

Cooking directions:

1. Break the chorizo apart and brown it in a large skillet.

2. Remove the chorizo into a bowl, leave the juices in the skillet.

3. Cook the onions in the skillet until soft.

4. Put back the chorizo, along with the salt and pepper, and diced tomatoes.

5. Allow to simmer for 10 minutes

6. You can either serve the zoodles dry or topped with sauce.

7. Before serving, you can sprinkle with parsley.

Day: 26

Chicken and Prosciutto Salad
(Ready in 30 minutes with preparation time of 10 minutes- serves 4)

Ingredients:

- 4 slices prosciutto

- 2 pitted, peeled and sliced avocados

- 4 tablespoons olive oil

- 1 thinly sliced red onion

- 12 chicken tenders

- ½ a cup sun-dried tomatoes (Drain if packed in oil)

- Spice of your choice (Ensure it is Whole30)

- 1 cup grape tomatoes

- 170 g baby greens

- Balsamic vinegar

Dressing

- 1 egg yolk

- Juice of 1 lemon

- 1 teaspoon minced garlic

- ½ cup olive oil

- Salt and pepper

Cooking directions:

1. Make the prosciutto crisp in a nonstick skillet, and then remove and chop coarsely.

2. Over medium heat, heat the oil in the skillet. Season the chicken with spice and then cook in the skillet until the chicken is well done.

3. Blend the olive oil, egg yolk, garlic, and lemon juice in a blender cup and then season with salt and pepper to taste.

4. Coat the greens with the dressing.

5. Serve with balsamic vinegar

Vegetable Bolognese with Eggplant Peppers, and Zucchini

(Ready in 55 minutes with preparation time of 10 minutes- serves 8-12)

Ingredients:

- 6 tablespoons olive oil

- 1 tablespoon dried basil or oregano

- 1 eggplant (peel and chop into ½ inch cubes)

- 3 cups tomato sauce (Ensure it is Whole30 compliant)

- 1 coarsely chopped onion

- 400 g diced tomatoes with juices

- 1 coarsely chopped red bell pepper

- ½ kg ground beef (or turkey)

- 1 coarsely chopped medium zucchini

- 1 teaspoon minced garlic

- Fine sea salt and freshly ground pepper

- ¼ cup beef broth

Cooking directions:

1. Heat 4 tablespoons of olive oil and add the eggplant then cook over medium heat for 5 minutes and remove from pan.

2. Heat the remaining 2 tablespoons and then add in the garlic, zucchini. Onion and bell pepper, then cook for another 7 minutes before you season with salt and pepper to taste.

3. Add the beef and cook thoroughly, keep stirring as it cooks.

4. Put back in the eggplant together with herbs of your choice, tomatoes and tomato sauce. Reduce the heat and simmer covered for 25 minutes. Check the seasoning and adjust if necessary.

5. Serve over zoodles of your choice.

Day: 28

Slow Cooker Taco Meat

(Ready in 250 minutes with preparation time of 10 minutes- serves3)

Ingredients:

- 1 kg grass fed ground beef

- ¼ teaspoon crushed red pepper

- 3 tablespoons tomato paste

- ¼ teaspoon paprika

- 1 tablespoon chili powder

- 1 teaspoon cumin

- ½ teaspoon onion powder

- 1 teaspoon sea salt

- ½ teaspoon dried oregano

- 1 teaspoon sea salt

- ½ teaspoon coriander

- 1 teaspoon black pepper

Cooking directions:

1. Mix all the spices in a small bowl.

2. Into the slow cooker put in the spice mixture, beef, and tomato paste. Break up the meat and with a spoon and also use it to mix the ingredients.

3. Cook for 4 hours on low. Keep breaking up the meat as it cooks.

Day: 29

<u>Roasted Coconut Oil Carrot Fries</u>
(Ready in 80 minutes with preparation time of 5 minutes- serves 2)

Ingredients:

- 1 kg fresh carrots (wash and cut into fries)

- ¼ cup coconut oil

- Sea salt and pepper to taste

Cooking directions:

1. Heat the oven to 350 degrees F.

2. Wash carrots and cut into strips like fries.

3. Coat the carrots in coconut oil by tossing them in coconut oil until fully coated.

4. In a sheet pan, spread the carrots, pour the leftover oil over them.

5. Sprinkle salt and pepper generously.

6. Roast for 45 minutes in the oven without opening the door.

7. After tossing the carrots, cook for another 30 minutes before serving.

Day: 30

Italian Salmon with Tomato Basil Salsa

(Ready in 20 minutes with preparation time of 5 minutes- serves 4)

Ingredients:

- 24 oz. boneless skinless salmon fillets

- 2 teaspoons olive oil

- ½ a teaspoon oregano

- ½ teaspoon dried basil

- ¼ teaspoon rosemary

- ¼ cup chopped basil

- ¼ teaspoon red pepper flakes

- 2 chopped tomatoes

- 2 tablespoons balsamic vinegar

- Salt and pepper to taste

Cooking directions:

1. Preheat the broiler.

2. In a small bowl, mix the red pepper flakes, basil, rosemary, and oregano.

3. Spray salmon with olive oil or cooking spray.

4. Use the spice mixture to season and also add the salt and pepper.

5. Toss pepper, salt, tomatoes, olive oil, basil and balsamic vinegar together and put on the side.

6. Broil the salmon for between 6 and 8 minutes. Salmon should be cooked through and flaky.

7. Use tomato basil salsa as a topping.

Conclusion

Congratulations for finishing our comprehensive guide so fast! We are sure that you must have had a great time preparing all these delicious meals.

To help you complete the Whole30 diet plan, we came up with a wide range of breakfast, lunch, and dinner recipes. In order to make things easier for you, we tried to experiment a little as well. We included various kinds of delicious recipes in our guide, so that you can complete the 30-day challenge without missing out on anything.

From avocado burgers to tuna salads and fajitas to smoothies, the guide covered a wide range of recipes. No matter what your requirements are, but you can definitely find something scrumptious to eat by taking the assistance of this comprehensive recipe book.

We have taken the overall intake of nutrients in mind while drafting this guide. This is to make sure that you would remain energized all day long while consuming these delicious meals. Also, you can prepare most of these recipes without spending a lot of time in the kitchen.

Additionally, we have walked an extra mile to educate you about the concept of Whole30 diet plan. From the basic dos and don'ts to the way you can prepare yourself, we have covered it all.

Nothing can really stop you now. Go ahead and complete the 30-day challenge to bring a positive change in your life.

Made in the USA
Lexington, KY
03 January 2017